Core Clear

SPIRITUAL CLEARING BASICS

JANE HAWK

Contents

Copyright

Earth Sun Union Press
an imprint of eXu Publishing
http://exupublishing.com/

Title: *Core Clear: Spiritual Clearing Basics*

by Jane Hawk

First trade paperback, hardback and eBook editions: May 2023

Copyright © 2023 by Jane Hawk and Earth Sun Union Press.

ISBN 13: 978-1-957125-09-1 (Paperback)

The author of this book does not dispense medical advice nor prescribe the use of any technique as a form of treatment for energetic, spiritual, mental, psychological, physical, or

Extended use license commercial use for spiritual bohemian clip art images by Lille Studio Los Angeles @LilleStudio. Pink, yellow watercolour image by Freepik. Sage bundle image by Vectonauta on Freepik. Sparkling pink fruit image, pink holographic blooming rose image, and floral wreath border glitter effect image by rawpixel.com. Watercolour frame image by rawpixel.com on Freepik and candle image by Freepik. Palm hand image by rawpixel.com on Freepik. All other images are licensed commercial assets from CreativeMarket or royalty-free or creative commons with commercial rights and no attribution required.

❁ Created with Vellum

Vibe your Dream Life

Note: *This book is dedicated to you and your spiritual clearing, dear reader, that inner work which is quite possibly the most challenging part of being human. To your every success in spiritual clearing, a necessary part of your vibing your dream life.*

Dedication

FOR DIANE

This book is dedicated to Diane (whose request and urgent need inspired the creation of the work) and to all those who have suffered with spiritual clearing and those who still do. May herein you find the tools and path to core clear your karma and any other negative (-) polarity material so that you might more easily vibe Your Dream Life—to your healing, beautiful souls.

To the Reader

Dear Modern Mystic:

Blessings and Congratulations to you! Thank you for downloading this eBook. The fact that you have taken action and are reading this now means you are taking responsibility for your Spiritual path. YOU are taking the initiative to purify your whole being (your mind, emotions, physical/kinesthetic and energy) and take responsibility for your karma, meaning your spirituality and life.

Before we get started, you should listen to me because I am a female shamanic practitioner, an energy healer, a creative coach trained in expressive arts for personal transformation, and a spirituality workshop facilitator with expertise in removing heavy or dark energy or energies, including entities, demons, attachments, as well as devices and implants. I have years of experience addressing my clients' psychic attacks and other spiritual and energetic issues.

This work evolved out of necessity and results from years of experience doing spiritual clearing work with the author, many clients, and a few friends and family. This book directly results from one client's desperate need and special request for practical at-home exercises she could do alone.

As you likely know, dealing with unpleasant spirit(ual) issues is expected, including psychic attacks, entities, dark forces, demons and other attachments, hexes and curses, or other draining and negative spirit(ual) experiences. Spiritual and energetic hygiene, like physical, emotional and mental hygiene, are necessary parts of being human. Many negative polarity experiences, including depression and low energy, irritability, obsessive and compulsive thoughts, and unpleasant emotions, including panic and fear, can be connected to a need to do spiritual clearing.

It can be costly to rely solely on a spiritual healer or shaman to do your spiritual clearing work. There is nothing like having a skilled, talented healer who can move energy, including attachments and other issues that block your Light. Still, there are many things you may find you can do yourself... in the privacy of your own home and this book, 'Core Clear: Spiritual Clearing Basics', will show you how. Of course, you can always reach out to your regular shamanic practitioner or other healer and have a session to resolve more complex or challenging issues (or if you feel you can't quite get the desired results yourself).

Yet you'll be amazed to discover that you can do a great deal of spiritual clearing for yourself with a bit of effort and the use of natural tools. In this short guide, you'll learn easy step-by-step tools and techniques to Spiritually Clear, purify your body and whole being, and change your life. The work is foolproof and employs cutting-edge transpersonal psychology, shamanic, energy clearing, and spiritual and new thought techniques and will bless your life for the better... forever.

Like all of our work and everything published by Earth Sun Union Press, this work has been created from the heart to help readers be their own guru so that they can vibe their Dream Life.

So much in life is about showing up rather than deserving. In reality and life, we often get what we are willing to work for to receive. With time, energy and intention, and the right tools and techniques, you can spiritually clear and get the results you want or need.

Making an effort, meaning taking action, is the key to

results. I have used these techniques to purify, meaning release demons, entities, dirty old stagnant energy, and dark forces taken on from others around us, including depressed, negative or dark people with addictions and other issues. Other techniques have been used to pull in or create beautiful energies and frequencies.

Energy is contagious; ever notice how you feel terrible after spending time around some people? Sometimes it's because entities, or other energies, jump ship and move from one person to another. Other times, energies, including entities and attachments, were latent in you all along, from karma, childhood trauma or ancestral issues, and being around a low vibe or negative (-) polarity person will stimulate those same frequencies from within you and bring things to the surface that you didn't know were there.

Fortunately, by acquiring this book, you now have an incredible arsenal of spiritual rituals to assist you in accessing, processing and releasing all that you don't want... everything low vibe or negative (-) in polarity.

I hope you enjoy and greatly benefit from these powerful spiritual clearing tools and techniques.

With blessings and love,

Jane Hawk

8

The Whole Being

How does spiritual clearing benefit a human or work? Spiritual clearing works by impacting some aspect of our human Whole Being. To understand the Whole Being, we must first consider the impact of energy medicine on ourselves and our reality.

At the subtlest levels, everything is energy, expressed in vibration as particles and waves. All forms are made up of subatomic particles. Quantum mechanics studies this area and is concerned with molecules, atoms, electrons and protons (made up of quarks held together by gluons), and other subatomic particles.

The yin-yang symbol represents how something can be both a particle and wave and illustrates how this reality runs along polarity continuums. Understand that everything is energy and that everything, including you, has a specific vibration and frequency.

Our uninjured Soul vibrates at the level of unconditional love, wisdom, peace, joy, generosity, kindness, and abundance, everything that is positive (+) in polarity. Our Soul's natural frequency is optimal for physical, emotional, mental and energetic health and well-being.

Our soul energy is exquisite, and if we can attune to our pure soul potential, the Divine aspect of our human self, we can vibe from a naturally abundant state.

The rest of our being, our Body, Mind, Emotions and Energy field, vibrates at a global frequency (GF) related to our particular karma, childhood wounding or trauma, and any painful or traumatic ancestral memory. This whole being GF = our life. We don't attract a particular life; we vibe it.

Frequency = Reality

All vibrations or vibes are primarily negative (-) or positive (+) in polarity. This includes our mental material (thoughts/fears/beliefs), emotional, physical/kinesthetic experience and energetic, which often means inner child, parallel life, or ancestral material. Indeed, some frequencies are close to neutral, yet, for this work, we are concerned with extremes in frequency.

Everything, every experience—and every expression in life—runs along polarity continuums from the highly negative (-) polarity to the extremely positive (+) polarity.

In a healthy person, the energy body generally is bright, has a vibrant emotional, energetic, and auric glow, and emits a high vibe or (+) polarity global frequency. When a person is depressed, ill or diseased (or when clearing negative (-) polarity material through spiritual clearing techniques), their global frequency is low vibe or negative in (-) polarity.

Again, some causes of negative (-) polarity are energy blockages or attachments or negative mental or ancestral issues, old trauma, or some combination of these or similar problems. Regarding a negative mental focus or attitude, a human may have negative (-) polarity mental material expressed through their personality as a bad attitude or negative (-) polarity personality. All negative (-) polarity material must be accessed, processed and released to return to a high vibe GF[1].

Soulular issue example: A child may have a Soulular pattern of biological matrilineal depression and despair related to a long-standing pattern, for women in that family, of accepting substandard, abusive and non-loving romantic relationships and partnerships. A being consciously on a Soul path will likely wish to examine and heal such a pattern.

The more severe health or other issues are, the weaker and less vibrant a person is as they are an extremely low vibe with a low or negative (-) global frequency. People at the end of their life—vibrate at the extreme end of the negative (-) polarity energetic continuum; this is natural as we transition from life to death. Our life force ebbs from our body as we start to pass away, and our soul prepares to leave the physical body and the physical realm.

Whole Being Material

Each of us has a whole being or global frequency. Life unfolds, and—depending upon the life plan we established from a Soul state before incarnating on this plane—we receive life lessons for our growth and evolution. After birth, we generally absorb some or all of our family and society's negative or limiting beliefs; we are often encouraged to fit in with the tribe. Additionally, we carry Soulular issues from our Soul lineages and connections with these individuals. Our reactions and responses to those life lessons, whether acceptance and humility, anger and bitterness, or the like, may create new karma.

After suffering intense pains or trauma, karmic in nature, as children or adults, we also may unconsciously block the natural flow of energy through our being by dissociating from our body and being and reality. Practically speaking, this means we are not entirely present to our experience, and then we do not process it emotionally, mentally, physically/kinesthetically or energetically.

Whole being material that we do not process in this or any other lifetime remains in our being at the cellular level.

What we do not process is generally negative (-) polarity experience or material. This material is typically deeply suppressed sadness, grief, shame, and other negative (-) polarity emotions, the emotional gunk residual from being abused or harmed, or as a side effect of being human and witnessing the terrible Soul crimes, war, rape, incest, murder, and so on, that are occurring on this planet.

When this (-) polarity material remains in our being at the cellular level, our global frequency or general vibe drops. This typically creates physical, emotional, mental and energetic problems, including disease, fatigue, stress and discomfort or pain and also affects or reduces our global frequency.

Processing your experience to maintain or improve your global frequency is vital. Tools and techniques to work through old trauma experienced in childhood or as an adult, ancestral memory, and spiritual clearing are crucial to increase your vibe. We can use primal scream, expressive arts therapies, journaling, hypnosis, and NLP, along with a great many other tools, to work through our whole being material that is negative (-) in polarity.

We can also increase our vibes by doing certain things.

High vibe expressions are obvious. We are generally naturally attracted to high vibe expressions.

High Vibe Life

To live a high vibe life, we must core clear all negative (-) polarity vibes and illuminate ourselves with high frequency or positive (-) polarity vibes. Most of us experience painful karma. It is an opportunity to learn, grow, and evolve mentally, emotionally and spiritually. We do not always take that opportunity, and many of us instead create new karma through reactivity.

Suppose we have resources, tools and techniques for transformation and the understanding that everything we experience results from our vibe. In that case, we can use karmic events to assist us in clearing old, sometimes ancient, karmic frequencies that equal our vibe at that same frequency (as the current life situation).

If you have health, wealth, and relationship issues, you have negative (-) polarity frequency or material issues. These create blocks to your whole being receiving wellness, abundance, or love because you are carrying and thus emitting low vibes.

Western science, and sometimes traditionally psychology, generally seems to focus on alleviating the symptoms or effects of imbalances or issues in a being.

The shamanic, spiritual clearing and transpersonal and energy psychology healing described here addresses the root cause(s), parallel life or Inner Child(ren), not the symptoms, of those issues.

High vibe frequencies or expressions—such as those one might sense from the watermelon tourmaline crystal pictured here—are beautiful to humans. Attraction to celebrities, or any other people, is often an attraction to their vibe (although we may be attracted to latent qualities within ourselves that we are projecting onto that person, or we can be drawn to the archetype or archetypes that the person is projecting at this or another time).

More simply, we are often attracted to someone because we wish to vibe at that same level of intelligence, wisdom, achievement, beauty, success, or power (or another attribute, ability or trait, whether singly or in combination).

You can increase your GF and be more high vibe by gratitude journaling, painting, meditating (when done correctly, not to self-medicate or escape), singing, dancing, gardening, or participating in other uplifting activities.

To change your life, you must, alone or with assistance, access, process, and release all energetic blocks and negative (-) polarity material and increase your global frequency through activities and actions that are high vibe.

Again, high vibe activities include meditation, prayer, chanting and making affirmations (when done correctly). You must fully embody or do the exercise with your whole being engaged, using your emotions, mind, and physical/kinesthetic experiences and energy.

One way to increase your vibe is to follow your heart and go toward what you are attracted to. If you love hiking and nature, then it is essential for you to pursue experiences in nature and to hike if you are able to do so without injury. If you love old coins or stamps, or baking, or gardening, or reading or writing, then you heal the world if you spend some of your time happily engaged in those pursuits.

Being Exquisitely Present

Being Exquisitely Present is the practice of focusing your awareness on your whole being experience, emotions, mind, physical/kinesthetic experience, and energy as intently as possible.

Other high vibe activities include gardening, playing, painting, or expressing your love of life and creativity. Focusing on being Exquisitely Present during an exercise such as this, as if your life depended on it, which it does, during such activities will dramatically increase your vibes. When you spiritually clear (remove what blocks your Soul light) and illuminate, your vibe goes up; you are more beautiful in every way because of the Light radiating from the core of your being.

Wholistic Life

you are beautiful

Life is complex. A life philosophy that is a unique synthesis of Eastern and Western philosophies with a heavy smattering of practicality may provide the most successful approach to moving from where you are to where you want to be.

There are tremendous benefits to using traditional or Western medicine and Eastern—meaning alternative and complementary and those like Traditional Chinese Medicine (TCM)—approaches combined in a holistic or wholistic manner.

Most issues should be addressed with every tool possible.

An issue manifested in the physical is quite severe; energetic shifts work at the subtlest levels of reality, and although, depending upon the person and situation, results may be pretty dramatic, it generally takes several months or more to see results in the physical.

One wouldn't attempt to take out the trash in your house by willing or intending that it be removed, meditating upon the situation, visualising the trash disappearing or imagining it floating through the air and being taken out, or positively affirming that the garbage would be taken out, would you? You would take it out or hire someone to do it.

If someone had a tumour, there could be a tremendous benefit, most likely, depending upon location, size and other information, for them to have it removed in addition to working with it energetically and shamanically!

Keep the power of a holistic approach in mind along your journey.

Some life issues may benefit from a more transpersonal and depth psychology approach, shamanic healing, including soul retrieval or journey work, or Inner Child consciousness work, such as Voice Dialogue. Generally, an aggressive holistic approach to handling an issue from all angles works best.

In the following sections of this book, you will learn exercises, tools and techniques for spiritual clearing and how to use those tools in sacred ceremonies or spiritual rituals at home to facilitate the clearing of energetic or other spiritual issues.

Altar Creation

You are invited to create a sacred space to prepare for your Core Clear inner work. Creating a personal sacred space is a significant first step in moving into ongoing, more profound personal inner work. It may be vital for the spiritual journey and your soulular development that you have an at-home altar, a private place to cultivate and worship all that is Holy, meaning the Divine masculine and feminine or G-d/G-ddess.

Being in the presence of your altar and spiritual space should be uplifting and joyful. An altar is a place to work with your energy, heal, purify karma, and Core Clear your material. A personal altar is a sacred place or space to sacrifice Low Frequencies or negative (-) polarity energies by releasing them to G-d/G-ddess and Mother Earth. It is also a place to set intentions, make offerings of flowers, and so on, and do more profound emotional healing like forgiveness work.

You can have little altars everywhere in your home; the kitchen is an excellent location for a tiny altar. A favourite mini altar location is

around an indoor plant; place little spiritual objects; perhaps a feather, crystal, or positive affirmation, an image, or spiritual ritual object, such as a shaman's rattle, a rose quartz or other tea light or votive candle holder (use vegan candles, when possible, as they are cruelty-free). You can keep spiritual tools in baskets under my altars.

The essences you may like to use may include plant, flower, gemstone or crystal, or animal (including bird) combinations or individual essences. Use the essences to stimulate the release of blocks to or evoke specific frequencies, traits or abilities.

Many spiritual practitioners generally use a table or shelf, or wooden altar, at a comfortable height and place a beautiful scarf or piece of fabric over it. Items are placed on top of the altar as touchstones, talismans that stimulate beautiful frequencies within one while we sit receptive, receiving, meditating, praying or talking to G-d/G-ddess.

Items used for a spiritual clearing ritual can be kept under the altar—on a wooden or other natural tray or

basket—and taken out only during a ritual. Be careful to avoid the use of artificial non-natural materials, and also DO NOT put items used in sacred ceremonies or spiritual rites on the ground (unless one is doing a holy ceremony or spiritual ritual in nature, where you may be using the earth alone or cloth-covered earth as your altar, such as in a Peruvian shamanic practice or similar).

Yes, Mother Earth is holy, yet she is also made up of dirt, which, when wet, becomes mud. The Pachamama ceremony is a sacred ceremony by the Andean people. This spiritual ritual involves worship of the feminine, fertile goddess, which they associate with Mother Earth, our planet. The Q'ero Inca Shamans, or the Qero, have multiple types of shamans working with various elements of reality.

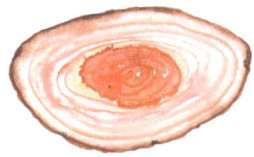

The Q'ero perceive the energy directed by the cosmos, called *Kawsay Pacha*, and the energy of Mother Earth, or *Pachamama*. The Q'ero know the value of spiritual and energetic clearing, as they believe that cleansing or clearing our energy field post trauma or other issues can prevent or heal illness

or other problems. Also, one must ground and bring in, be a container for, the energies of the planet and the cosmos.

Generally speaking, though, if you live indoors, and that is where you will do your regular, near-daily spiritual clearing practice, then we do not put our ritual items on the ground unless they are wrapped or contained in a shell, basket, or another receptacle.

Spiritual Tools

Spiritual tools are any items used for sacred ceremonies or spiritual rituals. These items should be set aside and kept in your altar or sacred space (the creation of this was described in the previous section). Many of these items, such as candles or sage, get used up, so they should be replenished regularly. Other things, such as crystals, should last a lifetime yet may need to be cleansed every so often (you can cleanse your crystals by holding them under running water and then putting them outside in the sunshine for several weeks).

- Salt
- Candles
- Incense
- Crystals
- Palo Santo
- Dried cedar
- Dried sage
- Essential oils
- Dried or fresh herbs/flowers
- Special or unique bath confetti
- Spiritual Images, including Yantra
- Prayers or Mantras
- Holy books (or prayers/poems)
- Sea shells or stones
- Pine cones, branches
- Abalone shell (to hold sage or cedar)
- Matches or a lighter* (to light candles or burn sage/cedar)

Your Inner Child or other subpersonality may love bath confetti; I've used batch confetti shaped like poodles, rose petals, hearts, and brightly coloured geometric-shaped ones for healing, to the delight of my Inner Child(ren). Objects like pine cones or branches shaped like runes make an especially meaningful altar and sacred space item. A photograph of a rose in a small frame can be helpful to evoke an embodied sense of your unique spiritual blossoming and unfolding. The image of a white flower or another pristine part of nature, such as a snowy landscape, can be placed in your sacred space so that you can meditate on this symbol of your increasing whole being purity.

You may like to connect with animal totems or messengers, or perhaps you have experienced synchronicity around the appearance of certain natural elements, animals, insects, or any other aspect of reality. Placing an image, carving, or figurine of such totems on your altar can be a way to amplify the attribute and meaning that the appearance of the symbol is intended to convey. Like past or parallel life issues or work, a symbol appears purely to evolve you spiritually.

*NOTE: Be careful, and stay safe! Keep your ritual and sacred ceremony items in a safe place (where children cannot find and use them).

Use of the Rituals

There is no doubt that preparation enhances the experience of a sacred ceremony. We would not attend a party or other celebration covered in dirt or sweaty and wearing rags. To prepare to use spiritual clearing tools, there are ideas that we can consider, such as the usefulness of tailoring spiritual rituals to one's unique perception of the Divine.

CREATE SACRED SPACE

We must first create a sacred space to use the spiritual or energetic tools available. Creating holy space involves choosing and creating the place or setting of your spiritual clearing practice.

Another way we create sacred space—when we are engaged in a spiritual ritual or sacred ceremony—is when we set aside space in time to do this valuable inner work. This means that before beginning your spiritual ritual, ensure you won't be disturbed.

It is ideal if you have a space set aside, a place used for no other endeavour to do inner work, including spiritual rituals.

Prayer, meditation, and spiritual rituals done in the same place will build up appreciable higher frequency energies over time.

When you create a special place, consider it an altar to the Divine within or without your Holy place or simply as your area to practice sacred self-care. In this space, put your items for clearing. A meditation or clearing space does not have to be large.

Remember to be flexible with yourself. Create your altar to reflect your own sense of Spirituality and Holiness, which honours your own Divinity within and without, above and below and all around.

I have used a closet with a small wood table and cushion, or a wooden box, or a meditation pillow in front of a table with wicker baskets, beautiful cloth or scarves, and crystals, flowers, or other holy items, on top (with sage, palo santo, herbs, incense, and other things, in a wood dish or small baskets nearby). Holiness is within and without; the divine within reflects the Divine without.

Being Exquisitely Present is focusing your awareness on the Whole Being experience (emotions, mind, physical/kinesthetic experience, and energy) as intently as possible. It is as if the experience or reality were something one wished to be present to with every molecule of their being.

~EXQUISITELY PRESENT

THE G-D/G-DDESS OF YOUR UNDERSTANDING

Replace G-d/G-ddess, or whatever is in the ritual or sacred ceremony, with the name of the G-d of your understanding. The Divine is masculine and feminine, as is humanity, so honour both in your spiritual rituals. Change the prayers and rituals to honour *your* path and unique spirituality and truth.

EMBODY & REVERE THE DIVINE

You want to access genuine reverence, love, gratitude, joy and awe for the essence of the Divine, so collect objects or things that facilitate those beautiful emotions.

When engaged in a sacred ceremony, remember to speak— aloud or inner audio—with humility and reverence; you are communicating with the Holy of Holies, the highest frequencies of all creation, and those Divine energies of human awareness and all creation. Remember to visualise as you pray, develop your ability to tune into and work with subtle energies, and maximise the experience.

DAILY REPETITION OF SPIRITUAL RITUAL WILL:

- Increase your frequency.
- Help you grow more energy sensitive.

- Develop/enhance your psychic abilities.
- Help you develop greater emotional and psychological balance.
- Give you tools to deal with difficult dark forces and energies.
- Strengthen your connection to and awareness of G-d/G-ddess.
- Allow access to ecstatic states, including love, peace, joy and bliss.
- Raise your global frequency (GF), blessing your Soul lineage and ancestry.
- Raise the frequency of, and thereby bless, the planet through your healing.
- Rewire your neurology, making accessing meditative and altered states of consciousness easier and easier.

Spiritual ritual isn't just about elevated frequencies and Holy emanations; it requires grounding refined energies into earthy reality. We must be a lightning rod between heaven and earth. We must be grounded on this planet and receptive to high vibe frequencies to do that.

When we do spiritual clearing and illuminating work, are spiritually clear and illuminated, we are made more beautiful, vibrant, light and life-filled.

In the next section, you will find an exercise to help you easily relax. When less tense or anxious, we can more easily ground into our bodies and be present to and in all reality. We must be present to receive, clear spiritually, and, of course, to *vibe our Dream Life!*

Relax the Body

Relaxing the body and being is critical. Regular relaxation, by getting enough sleep, avoiding overworking, and avoiding stressful situations and people as much as possible, is ideal. The exercise below can help you reset and relax before a sacred ceremony or spiritual ritual.

PREPARATION FOR THE EXERCISE

Breathe deeply. You may find yourself yawning and sighing throughout. Yawning is breathing with your mouth open. Breathing with your mouth open, or yawning, stretches and relaxes the facial muscles and will relax your body and being. Sighing is another way of relaxing. It brings feelings of relaxation and opens the heart chakra.

RELAX THE BODY EXERCISE

1. *Plant your feet.*
2. *Embrace your belly with your hands and arms. Breathe. Relax your head, and allow it to hang forward. Breathe.* (This provides a gentle, relaxing spine stretch.)
3. *Rotate your head. Breathe. Rotate your head in the opposite direction. Breathe.*
4. *Clench both hands into fists and stretch your arms before you, fists clenched. Breathe. Rotate your arms so the insides of your arms point up. Breathe. Relax your hands and them.*
5. *Touch your chin to your chest. Breathe for a count of ten. Sigh, and yawn if possible.* (Sighing combats stress, like yawning.)
6. *Tilt your head to the left (hold for a count of ten). Breathe. Tilt your head to the right (hold for a count of ten). Breathe.*
7. *Place your left hand on the back of your head, cupping your skull where your spine meets it. Put your right hand on your heart. Breathe for a count of ten.*
8. *Place your left hand on your forehead, cupping your skull above your eyebrows. Put your right hand on the back of your head, cupping your skull where your spine meets it. Breathe for a count of ten.*
9. *Place your attention on your third eye area (your Ajna centre) between your eyebrows. Breathe. Close your eyes and focus on that area for ten seconds.*
10. *Place your left hand on your heart and your right hand on top of your head. Gently tap your skull with the flat of your hand three times.*
11. *Place your right hand over your thymus at your high heart. Place your left hand on top of your right hand. Breathe.*
12. *Touch your wrists together with your hands cupped upward. Breathe.* (These actions anchor the exercise into our body and grounds us into the earth.)

Other ways to relax or increase our ability to relax include meditating upon a natural object or a photograph of a natural object. I don't use cut flowers because they are dying; they have been exploited for human consumption, which is not spiritual, meaning evolved behaviour.

ART AS MEDITATION

Instead, I meditate on a living plant growing in a pot or growing in nature. You can meditate upon a photograph of a rose, a willow tree, or some aspect of nature that fills you with energy. You can draw or paint plants, trees, or living things as a meditation or prayer; your intention with the act makes creating nature art a way to relax, meaning a meditation. Try the following destress meditation to ground and breath in and transmute your anxiety and stress.

DE-STRESS MEDITATION

Find a comfortable place to recline or sit where you will be undisturbed.

Very slowly, with as much intention as possible, starting at the top of your head, attune to every bit of tension and anxiety in your body.

Start with your head, being careful to sense into or attune to your face, ears and neck, moving downward to the rest of your body.

Feel the weight of the world, your cares, and everything that is causing you to feel tight, heavy, anxious, depressed, or despairing. Breathe into the tensions and any dark feelings or emotions or other sensations.

Associate as fully as possible to every aspect of your whole being, your emotional state, energy level, physical/kinaesthetic experience, and mental state.

Hold yourself, your body and your being gently, knowing that you will nurture and care for yourself as you grow and evolve as a lifeform on our Mother Earth.

Breathe your tension in and notice how it changes as you focus on the emotion and related sensations.

Attune as intently as possible to any upset, fatigue, and emotional pain, and notice how the negative (-) polarity experience dissipates—it slips away—the more attention that you give to the pain of your whole being.

Take a deep breath in and relax. Be certain to continue down from the core of your body and being, attuning to your torso, and any tightness, pain, and physical sensations associated with emotions or other whole being experiences.

Pay special attention to your limbs, arms, legs, hands and feet.

Breathe in your anxiety and pain, softening into it, relaxing, breathing deeply, until you are relaxed.

Take a moment to remind yourself of your courage, the challenge of being human and sensitive, and the need to appreciate and care for yourself.

Give yourself a hug; tell yourself how much you love and appreciate yourself.

You may like to repeat the destressing by associating to tension and pain exercise above each night as you fall asleep. As you core clear old stuck emotions and energy, your life force will move more freely and respond more powerfully to illuminate work. We need a strong connection to the planet to receive and hold energy, to release unwanted energies, and to be creative and well. In the next section, we will ground even more deeply into the body and strengthen our connection to Mother Earth.

Grounding

GET REAL; COME DOWN TO EARTH

Grounding means to make or strengthen your earth connection. You need to get and remain grounded to hold your energy and feel well physically and otherwise.[1] To maximise the benefits of your experience, do the prior body relaxation and this unique grounding exercise before each spiritual clearing ritual.

GROUNDING EXERCISE

1. *Sit in front of your altar. Take a deep breath in and release. Feel your rear against the floor or ground's surface, the cushion, or whatever you are sitting on.*
2. *Relax and breathe deeply, tuning in to your body and being.*
3. *With your Mind's Eye, see your energy flow, your Light and life force, chi or prana, flowing from your spine and throughout your entire body and being.*
4. *Visualise this energy, your Light, extending (from the top of your head and your crown down through your spine to your tailbone) as a cord of Light. Feel and see your cord of Light push against the surface you are sitting on.*
5. *Now feel into and experience this Light cord, from your crown through your tailbone to your spine, running down through the structure where you're sitting, continuing downward until it grounds with and connects with the earth. Experience and visualise this cord travelling through cement, rocks, and roots, whatever is beneath the structure you are in, connecting deep into the ground.*
6. *Relax even further, breathing more and more deeply relaxing as your energy cord almost tugs and connects you more deeply with a deeper, cooler part of the earth as if your energy was the roots of a tree, hungrily growing downward and connecting with the ground of Gaia, the Mother Earth.*

7. *Be aware of your energy cord continuing further downward, past earth elementals and other nature and natural beings, past caves and underground streams, magical fae realms and other miraculous places.*
8. *Breathe even more deeply as you feel your cord of energy, your being, body, and spine pulled deeply into the lava realms of the earth by the gravity of our planet. Feel and see your grounding cord move deep inward through the molten core until you feel into and reach the entirely grounding inner core of the earth.*
9. *Release anything that is not you into Mother Earth, intending that energy be released and purified in the core of the Mother, where it may then be pure lifeforce used to help and heal the planet.*
10. *Open your eyes.*
11. *Relax, and breathe deeply, feeling held, like a child, by Mother Earth.*

Other activities may help us to ground physically. Weight-bearing exercises, such as lifting actual weights, or walking in nature, may be earthing or grounding. Actually, soul retrieval work to regain lost parts of self (POS) may be required for you to become a more grounded, whole person. You should work with someone expert in this area or take shamanic training to retrieve your Soul parts. Also, know that parts, once retrieved, will need healing of the trauma(s), often intense, including possible abuse, which caused those parts to split off and dissociate from you originally.

Spiritual Ritual

Sacred ceremonies or spiritual rituals can be powerfully effective. The practices and exercises work in various specific ways. Our every action and activity impacts the molecules of our physical being, whether spiritual clearing or otherwise, and our emotions and energy can be affected by sacred ceremonies and spiritual rituals.

The Power of Spiritual Ritual

1. Spiritual rituals or sacred ceremonies all involve intention setting, the powerful act of preparing for and creating a ritual with the intent of purification.

2. Some of the exercises involve a body scan, using your Inner Eye, a higher chakra level ability, to look for dense energies, parallel life objects or karmic issues, demons, entities, or other beings or items, which will appear transparent or translucent, as you will be seeing them in the etheric (s).

3. The rituals generally involve removing—or facilitating the release and letting go of—energies and frequencies you do not want. This is a function of intention setting and energy healing work.

4. This work involves becoming intimately acquainted with your material, emotions, energy, thoughts, and physical/kinesthetic experience, which will attune you to what in your whole being is you and what is <u>not you</u>.

5. Spiritual ritual and exercises, particularly Psychosynthesis, encourages you to be Exquisitely Present, which will help you to access, process, and release (or assimilate or transmute) energies, as appropriate, that you have come into contact with, including Demonic or other Low-frequency energies. It also, along with grounding, helps you hold the beautiful, high frequency Divine energies you can attain through spiritual ritual.

6. Each sacred ceremony and spiritual ritual involves connecting with (for guidance, healing and transformation) non-ordinary reality. Non-ordinary reality is around us all the time. Still, most people are unaware of it except when they get an intuitive hunch, have a vision or precognitive dream, or hear a voice (although usually not a sub-personality or Inner Child) giving guidance. From a left-hemisphere perspective, the non-ordinary reality is the collective unconscious holding all archetypes of being. From a right-hemisphere perspective, non-ordinary reality holds all realms outside this one, including all parallel life realms and the Divine.

White Sage Ritual

Dried white wage (Salvia apiana) is a plant burned and used in spiritual rituals to transmute negative frequencies and dark energies. The use of the plant for this purpose may be relatively new; there do not appear to be historical records documenting its use before the 60s.

Some people mistakenly call the use of sage 'smudging'. They may tell you to 'smudge yourself'. Indigenous persons I have spent time doing sacred ceremonies with, including grandmothers from First Nations cultures around the world, indicate that smudging is a *negative term*. Smudge is a word which means dirty. The synonyms of smudge are blotch, smear, stain, mark and splotch. You are not smudging or dirtying yourself when you burn sage and use the smoke to clear yourself or facilitate your clearing. You are saging yourself for purification.

White sage can be expensive. It grows primarily in Southwestern California and has likely been overharvested. Grandmother Biliwara Lee, from Australia, taught me that you could also burn wormwood to clear dark energies. Other indigenous grandmothers have taught me that one can burn dried cedar or palo santo wood sticks. You can add dried lavender or other dried flowers for additional frequency healing or purification.

If you harvest anything from the land, you should leave an offering, preferably corn meal or loose organic tobacco, though your saliva or strands of your hair will do if you have nothing else on hand. As you leave the offering, make a prayer and express or intend appreciation to and for the earth.

Mother Earth is the Divine feminine—she makes all life possible—and deserves great honour. An offering is a way to express Gratitude and Love for Spirit, the Earth, and the item or items you harvest.

So pick and dry, or purchase, some organic sage leaves or a bundle, preferably containing some White Sage. Please place it in an abalone shell, beautiful pottery, or another fireproof dish. If you use a shell, create a liner made of aluminium foil doubled for strength and almost as shallow as the container. The foil in the shell or container will catch ash; you can also wrap your shell up in different foil so that you might take it with you as needed.

All things, including people and objects, may take on energy from other existing items. A sage ritual is an excellent way to purify your energy as part of, or before, a spiritual clearing ritual.

WHITE SAGE RITUAL

Sit in front of your altar.

Contemplate the white sage momentarily, and call forth the essence of the deva, the elemental Soul of the sage plant leaves. You may see her.

Express your most profound gratitude to the deva or Soul of the sage (and any other plants or herbs).

Light the tips of the sage leaves or bundle. Once they are burning, blow the flames out with a feather, feather fan, or gentle breath.

Once lit, do not stop it from burning/smoking unless you absolutely must, as the sage will sense the degree of purification and cleansing required and burn appropriately.

Carefully place the lit smoking leaves or bundle of sage in the abalone shell or container.

Holding the shell or other container, gently waft the smoke and sage your entire body and being.

Set the intention to, and visualise, the sage transmuting the low vibes in/around you. Intend that all negative (-) polarity frequencies move downward, grounding into Mother Earth and being released from your body and whole being.

You may feel lighter after saging. Saging may cause a considerable clearing reaction.

If you are saging and need to release or are releasing lots of heavy energies, darkness, dark entities or otherwise, your bundle or branch of sage may burn and smoke a great deal... maybe entirely until the entire bundle is ash.

When you are done, set the container on a kitchen stove or fireplace hearth. Sage burns hot when fired up.

Thank the Spirit of the sage when you are done.

NOTE: *Be safe* meaning *do not have fans on or windows or doors creating drafts when using sage in ritual.* Keep paper, long hair, and flammables near or around your altar away from the sage.

If you are saging to clear sticky energies that you may have picked up or for any other reason, be careful to sage your entire person. To do this while standing, you can stand on one foot and sage under the foot you are holding up and then switch sides; sage the front and back of your body, above your head and both palms. Be careful to sage around your spine and tailbone, your grounding connection to Mother Earth.

Sage before clearing rituals and anytime you feel negativity (sage all objects/belongings and your entire space regularly).

Periodically sage your living space, your automobile, and most objects you purchase or otherwise receive. Purify daily and practice gratitude to the spirit of the sage for transmuting lower frequencies.

Bath as Ritual

Water is a great conductor of energy. It makes releasing negative (-) polarity material or unwanted vibes easier. A relaxing temperate bath filled with herbs and crystals and a ritual for spiritual clearing are fantastic. The steam of warm or hot water will allow the fragrance of essential oils or dried flowers to waft upward and bless and heal your whole being.

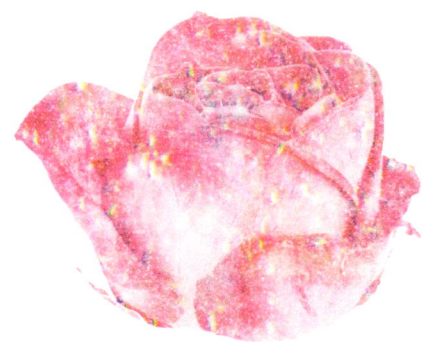

Planning a spiritual clearing bath is a lovely gift for yourself. You can get excited about gathering the items that will make your bath joyful and unique. Essential oil combinations can powerfully boost spiritual clearing work; Young Living (http://youngliving.com/) has some of the best essential oils and blends available[1].

Buy some lavender at a farm stand, outdoor market, or elsewhere. You can hang the bundle in your kitchen, decorated with a bit of ribbon and bougainvillaea or other flowers, where you can grab some for your bath or to burn with a bit of sage.

BATH RITUAL PREPARATION

Gather the items you need for your bath.

Use salt, herbs or flowers (dried or fresh), essential oil, and even crystals if you feel you have particularly dark material to release.

Make sure to have towels and a robe, and slippers nearby.

You might like to listen to meditative or uplifting music or a guided visualisation while in the bath (if you want to do so, then—along with selecting other needed ritual bath items— get the required music or other things in advance).

You might like to have a prayer or mantra to repeat in the bath, listen to a guided visualisation on MP3, or focus on a spiritual image. You can use a laminated copy of the Kabalistic Cleansing Prayer (from this book) for the bath ritual. You can tape it to the wall of a shower or bathtub and meditate upon it, spiritually clearing, as you soap and rinse each day.

If your Inner Child is traumatised and abused and fears life— because you were abused as a child, a victim of war or another horrendous fate—finding your connection to the Holy source of all being can be powerful. Try viewing images of beautiful nature, such as a framed photograph of a perfect rose and statues of deities that you experience as expressions of G-d/G-ddess.

If you plan to meditate upon a particular prayer or image that uplifts you—or helps you release dark energies or related material—then place that near the bath.

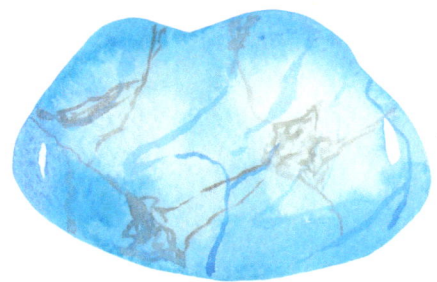

SPIRITUAL CLEARING BATH

Create your bath altar to spiritually clear the temple of your body by lighting candles and incense and placing flowers or petals around your bath.

Firmly set the intention to uplift your body and being, and Spiritually Clear by the bath ritual you are about to take. Sprinkle the salt, some herbs or flowers (or bath confetti for a healing Inner Child bath) and several drops of essential oil in the bath[2].

When ready, enter the bath, allow yourself to sink into the warmth and experience negative forces flowing from you. Visualise and imagine the salt drawing out low vibes and negative (-) polarity energies, including old past trauma and abuse(s) experienced.

Meditate, pray, relax and allow the energies and visuals of the flowers, herbs, crystals, petals, and candlelight to uplift and heal your being.

When you have finished, stand and rinse yourself well with warm water. Envision the water washing away any remaining heaviness or other negative (-) polarity frequencies.

Get out and gently wrap the temple of your body in a bath towel.

Dress and, if possible, get in bed, nap, or sleep.

Dark Force Entity Release

This exercise, written by myself, is inspired by the Psychosynthesis body of transpersonal psychology and spiritual work created by Robert Assagioli. Psychosynthesis helps synthesise the Lower and Higher selves[1] and our Parts of Self (POS) or subpersonalities to resolve inner conflict and release material and blocked energy. See books by Hal and Sidra Stone to learn more about POS. The idea behind the work is that humans naturally self-reorganise when blocks are removed.

Psychosynthesis exercises elicit profound transformation and wholeness, integrating your disparate personality and other aspects. The work impacts your whole being, affecting your emotions, thoughts, energy, and physical/kinesthetic and Spiritual experience. Daily or long-term repetition of this, or any psychosynthesis exercise, like all spiritual rituals, enhances the benefit.

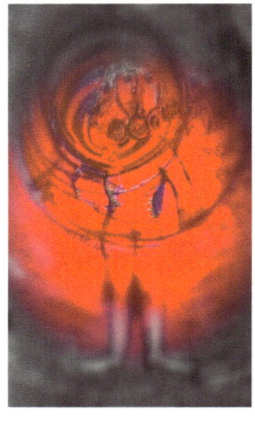

In this work, we return Demons, and all Dark Forces, to their next highest evolution with our love and blessings, trusting that Source, G-d/G-ddess, the creator of all, will restore beings to the proper place. In one real sense, there is no other place to put them. At the unified field level of reality, all is connected... we're all one.

In this work, we do not merely release demons. *All things come from G-d, and all things may return (though the level to which they return may not be an upper realm).* If there is such a thing as forgiveness, all beings, energies and frequencies have an equal chance at redemption.

If you like, you can record the process in your voice and then do the exercise without being forced to read it.

Prepare for the exercise.

Quiet yourself.

Sit in a comfortable chair or on a couch (lying down), and allow your eyes to softly nearly close—keeping them open just enough to read this exercise—and relax.

Allow yourself to breathe deeply and regularly.

Take a deep breath in, and let that breath out with a yawn, an awh sound or a sigh.

DEMONIC RELEASE RITUAL

Imagine that it is dusk. You are in a meadow. Become increasingly aware of your environment—strain to see the landscape around you. The air is pleasant, and the last of the sun's rays shoot gorgeous red, orange and gold light across the sky. There is soft green grass on the ground beneath you.

Be aware of your feet making contact with the earth and your clothing. Listen to the sound of a gentle breeze. Somewhere in the distance, you hear thunder rumble.

As the sky grows darker, the air becomes a bit cooler. Become clearly aware of the landscape around you.

Feel something shift within you. Sense your determination and willingness. As you examine your surroundings, notice a nearly hidden path leading into the woods.

The woods are dark; gazing at them, you sense an almost imperceptible movement inside them.

Intrigued, you determine to enter the woods. You take several steps and find yourself inside. It is pleasant.

You can smell the earth and the scent of trees and growing things in this place. You make your way, thinking perhaps you are lost as there isn't really a path, just the hint of a trail.

As you get deep into the forest, you pass, and in the darkness, you almost don't notice a pile of boulders. You recognise a cave and enter it.

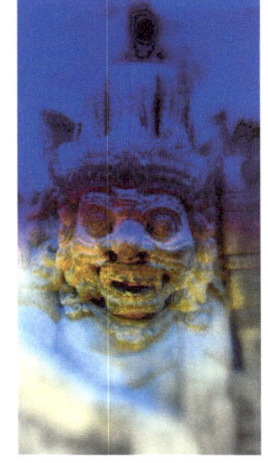

The ceiling is low, but you manage to scramble, using your hands and arms, over rock until you reach the back of the cave. There is an opening there and markings on the walls. You feel the holiness of this place and know that you have found a temple within. You enter the opening in the earth.

You can't see much; somewhere, there must be a tiny opening. Moonlight shines. The air is still here, and there is no movement at all. It appears as if the tunnel ends. You pause for a moment and catch your breath.

Hearing a slight noise, you touch the wall before you and notice an opening after all. You enter the opening, and the moonlight grows brighter. You have entered a cavern. Moonlight, blue in the darkness, glistens on the walls and rocks here. Ancient statues and powerful deities stand silently guarding this place.

In the centre of the cavern is a seat made of stone. There are more strange markings on the walls and primitive images. You instinctively know to seat yourself. As you do, you relax further and fall into a light trance.

The shadows grow larger. You sense movement. You see images of red and black through your nearly closed eyelids, like figures in the movement.

You breathe even more deeply and notice there is a movement within you, throughout your body and being. You relax entirely and see that the figures you can see more clearly now are inside or connected to your body and being. You acknowledge their presence.

You explain that you are revoking all vows and contracts with dark forces, satanic and separates, including demons, demon fragments, and demon eggs and egg sacks. You ask them to return to Source.

Something within you rumbles, and there is a shift.

Energies, being, and frequencies begin to move upward through your chakras, and being, and out your mouth, the crown of your head and body.

You sit, breathe deeply and allow the release to happen. The movement waxes and wanes and the release occurs in waves.

It is very dark here, but you accept that.

Energies flow in fragments and larger pieces. You may see, hear, or otherwise experience them; you allow them to depart.

If necessary, you dialogue with any dark force that doesn't want or is afraid to leave. You explain that it must; calm any fears it may have about going out and up and to its next highest evolution. Explain the nature of karma and that it may reincarnate. You notice you have extraordinary compassion for these beings, many of whom have been with you for thousands of years.

Some of them seem angry; for the most part, they seem to depart without trouble. You notice one or more parallel lives where you invoked them or were otherwise contaminated. You send them into the Light with your love and blessings.

Sometime later, you notice that, at this time, you are complete.

You take a deep breath, open your eyes and stand up. The air in the cavern is more refined. Something has changed dramatically. You take a step and notice you feel very different, lighter. With a sigh of relief, you turn and see that there is a back way out.

Outside light faintly illuminates the cavern exit. You quickly make your way toward and through it. You find yourself in a tunnel with a steep incline. You exert your muscles and move rapidly upward.

You see a narrow opening at the top of the incline that you can squeeze out of. You squeeze through and find yourself in the meadow. The flowers smell faintly sweet, like honey.

Light spills like liquid across the scene. This Holy Light enters you and fills every opening that was left by the now-gone dark forces. Dawn has broken, and you realise you were in the cave far longer than you thought or experienced yourself to be.

The morning sun on the meadow creates a breathtaking scene.

You turn and notice that you can no longer see the cave opening. The air is fresh. You breathe it in deeply.
You notice bees on the meadow flowers.
You can almost feel their wings hum.
The flowers smell like honey.
Everything seems sharper and fresher.

You take a moment to thank the Holy one, the creator.
You focus your awareness.
You notice you feel joy and a lightness you haven't felt before.
Take your time to experience your new lightness of being.

Energy Cord Detangling

Your chakras are energy centres through which your life force—prana or chi—flows freely if things function correctly. Meaning energy should flow freely, though other issues can create blockages. The flow of your life force and how much energy you generate and allow to flow freely through your being affects your global frequency or overall vibration or vibe.

When healthy and in balance, your chakras are open, each spinning in the appropriate direction for your gender and sexual orientation and balanced while your energy flows freely.

Upper chakras correspond more to the subtle realms. Lower chakras have more to do with elemental realms and earth functions like survival.

Part of gaining and maintaining energy is by being grounded to the earth and receiving energy or power from Source, G-d/G-ddess, and other origins.

We want to be like a flower, rooted or grounded in the earth, having our energy cycle through our being. We must be grounded to hold our energy. We get energy by eating/drinking when our body metabolises those substances and by exercising or resting. We get energy when we are positive (+) polarity in emotion.

When we are happy, excited, and joyful, we are energised. We get energy by being receptive. We can get energy by taking in beautiful or positive (+) vibes by looking at nature—and taking in natural vibes energetically—or by listening to and taking in more with our bodies than our heads, the vibes of beautiful music or art. Everything is vibration.

It is vital to master your energy and thus avoid talking excessively or otherwise expending excessive energy.

Generally, you want to accrue more energy than you expend.

We can lose energy by being entangled or energetically and other-wise codependent with people. This happens when we have an unhealthy connection with someone. Energetically we are corded to them, and some of our energy flows to them.

You may be doing things for someone because you cannot say 'No.' Most likely, you have previously had an experience where you felt your energy drop after being around someone needy and demanding.

You may know or have previously known someone who is or was energetically predatory. Like an energy vampire, an energetically predatory person is someone who drains you any time that you are around them.

Energy Cord Clearing Preparation

In this exercise, you will scan your body and being and pull the cords if you see lines of energy connecting your chakra and being to someone else.

Quiet yourself.

Sit in a comfortable chair or on a couch (lying down), and allow your eyes to close, keeping them open just enough to read this exercise, and relax; allow yourself to breathe deeply and regularly.

CHAKRA DETANGLING EXERCISE

Beginning with the crown of your head, scan your body and whole being with your mind's eye, examining your chakras one by one to see if there is one or more that has a cord or cords connected to it.

Use your hands by waving them gently in front of each chakra; if entangled, the energy area in front of that chakra will feel sticky. You may or may not be able to see, feel, or otherwise sense the tangled chakra cords.

When you find a cord or cords of energy to remove from a chakra, allow your mind's eye to present an image or otherwise reveal to you (you may know or hear that person's name) the person or people corded to you in this area.

Take your hands, grasp the cord(s) of energy, and gently, yet firmly, pull them out of your chakra and body. Just like a weed in your garden, you want to be sure to remove all the roots and threads of energy.

Firmly and gently pull and remove the cord(s). If the lines of energy extend into other chakras, draw out and remove those cords and subtle energy threads until the area no longer feels sticky.

During or after this process, you may have emotions or thoughts about a specific person, group, or event. Remind yourself to journal about or consider this later.

When the cord or cords—threads and all—have been removed, you can release send the residual sticky or other energies down into Mother Earth to be purified and feed the planet with your love and blessings... requesting that it be restored to its highest evolution for the highest G-d/G-ddess of all concerned.

Use your mind's eye to see if cords of your personal energy are inappropriately attached to other beings in any way. Pull them back to you if they are. Hopefully, your energy lines are clear and light, but purify them anyway.

As your energy comes back into your body, use your right hand to direct light or energy from the Soul Star in your palm at the energy and purify it entirely.

Use that same hand to direct light and heal wounds or holes (if any) from where you removed cords of energy previously tangled in your body and being.

Repeat the process, as necessary, moving through all of your chakras.

Remember to check the back of your body. People can also be corded to chakras on that side of the body.

Take a moment and check your root chakra, ensuring your energy is grounded in the earth.

With your mind's eye, examine the energy running in your chakras.

If it feels imbalanced, stuck or stagnant in any way, use your hands and intention (and request assistance from your spirit animals or totems if you wish) to remove any etheric objects, stuck energy blobs, blocks, etc.,

Send denser energies that you find down into Mother Earth (through your grounded spinal cord and spine).

Sage yourself... and your space. Pay particular attention to where you removed and released cords from others or other energy.

Smooth your entire energy field and aura, starting from your crown.

Take a moment to thank G-d/G-ddess and any animal messengers or helpers who may have assisted you in this process.

Remember to drink lots of water after doing this exercise.

If you feel ungrounded, do the grounding ritual or something to stimulate your left hemisphere and ground you into reality. You might like working on a financial spreadsheet, checking e-mail, cleaning a bathroom, or organising files.

Relax the Body

As with previous spiritual clearing work, it is recommended that one begins by doing first the relaxation or Relax the Body exercise and then the Grounding exercise from earlier parts of this book. Then, when relaxed and grounded, continue with the ritual below.

Pre-Ritual Intention

Light a candle with great reverence, setting the intention to cleanse your being at the deepest levels as is for the highest G-d and G-ddess of all concerned.

Sage your entire self, including under your hands and feet (lifting each foot to sage beneath it).

PARALLEL LIFE CLEARING RITUAL

Sit at your altar and light incense to honour G-d and G-ddess and your animal helpers and in honour of the clearing they will assist you with.

Be sure to make all prayers with the greatest devotion,
humility and sincerity you can muster.

Invocation

Mother/Father, G-d/G-ddess, Grandmother/Grandfather (or Great Spirit or the G-d of your understanding), I focus my attention on the sparkling, pure Light of Divinity flowing through me and into me from Source, above my crown chakra.

I invite my animal helpers, never reprogrammable by the dark, to be with me and assist me in this healing and clearing. I ask you to please help me to access, process, and release all energies, entities, and attachments, and all frequencies and molecules below neutral, that are blocking Light for me. I ask that transformation be allowed simultaneously in all bodies, times, realms and dimensions, as is karmic-ly neutral or beneficial and for the highest G-d of all concerned. Gratitude and love to you for your service.

I invite you in and ask to be surrounded by the essence of the highest Divine vibration possible. I request that energetic adjustments and re-calibration for my highest G-d/G-ddess be made as necessary, and I thank you.

I ask that the essence of G-d/G-ddess (The G-d of your understanding as is preferred) consciousness surround me and all parts of self, being and expressions and that we are held safely and protected in this work. I ask that I be protected from false guidance and that truth be revealed in my experience.

And Adonai/Shekinah, Divine, Holy Source of all being, let this clearing be karmically *neutral*, or beneficial, to me with harm to none and no negative karmic consequences to any.

And I ask to be *entirely surrounded* by the highest frequency love and Light of Source, Adonai and Shekinah, and completely protected from any energies and beings, in any form, realm, time and dimension, and that they be returned to the Light, the G-dhead, as is for their own highest evolution.

Shekinah, from you, all things emerge, and all things return; please bless this healing work and allow me to feel your Love and Blessings. Kadosh (Holy), Shekinah. Thank you for bringing the body of G-d/G-ddess into my being so that, like him/her, I may shine with my unique Divinity.

I ask that you consecrate and make Holy this healing. Thank you for the Light and Love, guidance, healing and protection. So it is, and so I am.

Baruch Shem Kevod Malchuto La'olam Vaed (Blessed is G-d's glorious majesty forever and ever).

Many thanks, Many Blessings. Amen.

Prayer

I ask G-d/G-ddess, above and below, within and without, and all around, interpenetrating all of my Being, my Higher Self, and all of Reality to clear me, my room, my family (partner with permission, and children under eighteen), my home, business, property, animals, belongings and possessions, and all parallel life selves and their Inner Children, and all Parts of Self and my Inner Children, of all disincarnate entities, all dark forces, all separates, all satanic energies, and all negative thought forms whatsoever, including vows and curses by and to me, across all lifetimes, in all times, realms and dimensions, and timelines, here and now, in the past, present and future, with harm to none and no negative karmic consequence(s) to any...

(*Go slowly with this, softening your gaze and scanning your body and being in your mind's eye, and using your hands as necessary, to assist the release of energies, entities, or any other dark attachment from your body, being and aura.)*

I, _____, for myself, and my relations, and all my incarnations, release all attachments, attractions, repulsions, contracts, vows and energetic connections to dark forces, and sources of darkness, pain, evil, illness, or any harm, and forgive them and release them and ask that I/we be forgiven.

We trust G-d/G-ddess (Spirit) to include all that we have failed or neglected to include in this clearing, here and now, with harm to none and no negative consequences to any, as is for the Highest G-d/G-ddess of all concerned, and we Thank You for this.

Thank you, G-d/G-ddess, Thank you, G-d/G-ddess, Thank you, G-d/G-ddess.

Devocation

I thank you, Divine Holy Source, Adonai and Shekinah[1], G-d/G-ddess, within and without, above and below, and all around; thank you for this healing and transformation. My Gratitude and Love to the Essence of all Divinity and Spirit Animals and any beings of Light who assisted me in this healing and clearing.

And I thank you, Light of G-d/G-ddess, Divine vibration, and all Beings of Light and Divinity, for your gifts and blessings.

And so it is, and so I am.

Baruch Ha Shem (Blessed be the Name).

Shekinah, Mother, and Adonai, Father, stay with me in the union of all things.

In your names, G-d/G-ddess, the Most Holy on High, Kadosh, Kadosh, Kadosh, (Holy, Holy, Holy)[2], Baruch Shem Kevod Malchuto La'olam Vaed (Blessed is G-d's majesty, forever and ever).

I pray that this sacred process be manifest with Grace and Love for the Highest G-d/G-ddess of all concerned.

And I close for now with Love and Peace and Ease and Grace. Amen.

After this parallel life cleansing or clearing ritual, sage yourself and the entire area around your altar and wherever else seems appropriate. Do so with the consciousness that you are transmuting, purifying and restoring to G-d/G-ddess all frequencies and energies, entities or otherwise, that were released from you and restored to the Light and their next highest evolution.

Remember to drink plenty of water and, if possible, take extra time to rest or nap.

There are many spiritual clearing and illuminating tools available from religions worldwide. Kabbalah means to receive or to be receptive. Kabbalah is an esoteric and ancient mystical tradition or aspect of Judaism. You do not need to be Jewish to use the spiritual illuminate or clearing tools available via Kabbalah. Join me in the next section, where you will find another cleansing exercise, a Kabbalistic purification prayer.

Note: Prayers do not need to be a form of cosmic begging or plea to the celestial realms, yet rather could be thought of and practised as a blessing, a meditation, an intention setting, and even be repeated as a chant. Please know that regularly employing the prayer practice—more frequent use—increases the cumulative positive energetic power and impact of the cleansing devotional. See you in the next section, beautiful Soul.

Cleansing Prayer

There are different ways to use prayer. This prayer is meant to be a meditative chant to elicit a unique spiritual cleansing in one's body and whole being. The Kabbalistic prayer in this section—provided to me by a Kabbalist in Los Angeles, CA— can be used ritualistically to release anything from your body and whole being that blocks your Light. You do not have to be Jewish to use Kabbalistic or Jewish spiritual tools. This prayer is the English transliteration of—meaning how you pronounce—the words of a Hebrew prayer.

KABALISTIC CLEANSING PRAYER

Kuma Adonay Veyafutzu Oyvecha, Veyanusu Mesanech Mipanecha.

The meaning of these words is:

Arise, Lord, and let your enemies be scattered, and the conquest of the land become instantaneous.

You can say Kuma Adonai (Addonay), or Kuma Ha Shem (Ha Shem means 'The Name'). Adonai means Lord or G-d, and Kuma means arise. The words may sound violent and might not seem spiritual until you understand the prayer's esoteric and alchemical purification meaning.

What the prayer means is:

Arise Lord within, my Higher Self, my Soul, eternally connected to the Divine (G-d/G-ddess), and let your enemies (these low frequencies, demons, attachments, dark forces, etc.) be scattered (from me released, transmuted, purified and restored to the essence of Divinity) and the conquest (spiritual clearing) of the land (myself/my body temple, my physical, energetic, mental, and emotional, and spiritual being) be instantaneous.

Like a mantra, you can repeat the prayer while visualising the release of all you are dealing with now. Do the body relaxation and grounding exercises before doing this exercise. During and following the exercise, communicate with the essence of Divinity and request that any entities, forces or dark attachments be restored to their next highest evolution for the highest good of all concerned, as is karmically neutral or beneficial for you.

Request that these energies, all molecules and frequencies, be transmuted into the pure white Light of Divinity, never reprogrammable by the dark. Now and forever. Hallelujah.

Follow this by saging yourself, taking a cleansing bath, or doing the complete sage ritual.

Hebrew name of G-d Meditation

Hebrew mystics and Kabbalists use one or more of the 72 Names of G-d (and permutations of it) in meditation for Spiritual transformation, including cleansing and purification of the body, mind, emotions, personality, and spirit. The Tetragrammaton is the four-letter or quadriliteral name of G-d made up of the Hebrew letters Yod, Hey, Vav, and Hey. Tetragrammaton literally means 'the four letters'. Per the Kabbalah Centre, 'The Tetragrammaton represents the totality of everything' (https://www.kabbalah.com/en/articles/the-power-of-the-tetragrammaton/).

This is the Ineffable Name or Unutterable Name of the G-d of Israel, the Creator. A human may purify and evolve their consciousness through meditation upon the Hebrew letters of The Name. This name of G-d—sometimes referred to as Ha Shem—meaning The Name, is Holy. The Name has innate holiness and can be considered a spiritual gift to evolve your Soul. If displayed on your altar, this word must be treated with appropriate reverence (and neither damaged nor mistreated).

Frame The Name and keep it covered, with lace or another special altar cloth, when you are not meditating upon it. Reminder, we do not utter—by which I mean pronounce—the Sacred Name to avoid desecrating it.

Read from right to left, no one knows how to pronounce the sacred Name of G-d (and, again, we should not try to speak or otherwise pronounce The Name).

Scholars suggest that the letters derive from the Hebrew verb 'to be' or hayah and surmise that this indicates that G-d, Divinity in its masculine form, is the transcendent Source and expression of all being. The word אֶהְיֶה ('Ehyeh) is the first person singular imperfective form of הָיָה (hayah), 'to be', and owing to the peculiarities of Hebrew grammar, means 'I am' and 'I will be'[1].

Meditate upon the image of the Tetragrammaton if desired (meditation instructions are below). Keep in mind that you must not be cavalier about the use of The Name in print or otherwise; if you copy or print The Name—or remove the page from the book that contains The Name in print—the Tetragrammaton must be disposed of properly if you ever decide to discontinue use of The Name. Please note, as detailed at the end of this section, that the printed Hebrew name of G-d, one of the 72 names, is Holy and thus should not be destroyed or otherwise misused.

HEBREW NAME OF G-D MEDITATION

1. Begin the Meditation

Sit comfortably, with the name of G-d, in a frame, on your alter. Take several deep breaths and, if you have them, light a candle and incense in honour of G-d.

The meditation consists of focusing on the Name while breathing in Light from within and around the actual Hebrew letters.

2. Focus your Attention

Try a soft gaze (allowing your eyelids to drop) to help you access an altered state of consciousness and focus your awareness on The Name.

3. Take a deep breath in.

Concentrate on envisioning and breathing in Light emanating from within and around the Hebrew letters.

Allow yourself to both feel and see the Light, which is emanating directly from the letters that spell The Name. Breathe in the FIRE from the letters and feel the Light radiating into your body, energy field and being.

4. In closing:

Express your deepest gratitude to the Divine, G-d/G-ddess, for the Light and your Life.

NOTE: As described here previously, the name of G-d is kedushah or holy, so it requires special treatment. A word for holy items is 'shaimos'; shaimos means names. The name of G-d, Hashem, in print, should not be abandoned or destroyed (it must be buried in Holy ground, meaning a Jewish cemetery to be appropriately disposed of per halacha or rabbinical law). Halakha also transliterated as halacha, halakhah, and halocho, is the body of Jewish religious laws derived from the written and Oral Torah. *Shaimos* refers to the names of G-d that the Torah prohibits erasing (you can learn more in the Torah in *Devarim* 12:2-4 or in the Talmud in *Shavuos* 35a).

In the article *Proper Disposal of Holy Objects* on Chabad, Rabbi Menachem Posner shares that, 'In many places, synagogues and other communal organisations arrange burial for items requiring it, at times asking for a fee to help defray the associated cost' (https://www.chabad. org/library/article_cdo/aid/475304/jewish/Proper-Disposal-of-Holy-Objects.htm). So, if affiliated, you might reach out to your local synagogue to properly dispose of a Holy item such as the Tetragrammaton printed name of G-d. Otherwise, you could seek shaimos disposal for a fee at https://chayenu.org/product/shaimos-box/. You can read more about the proper disposal of shaimos items at https://www.ok.org/article/mountains-of-shaimos/.

Aura or Auric Hygiene

These aura rituals (one for clearing and one for healing) are easy and fantastic. You can do it almost anywhere. An aura clearing is a tremendous spiritual clearing ritual to do each time you go to the bathroom, particularly if you live in a city and work or interact with many people.

It is possible to do this exercise around many people, very casually, as if you were brushing something off of yourself as—if you make subtle movements—the people around you are likely to remain oblivious.

First, gently rub the palms of both hands together to activate the soul star in the centre of each palm.

These soul stars are often described as eyes in the palms in esoteric texts or art. However, the soul stars look more like tiny suns to me. During the self-clearing, use your mind's eye or inner vision to visualise or see or scan your energy field while sensing with your hands.

AURIC CLEARING EXERCISE

1. Standing relaxed, breathing as deeply as possible, stretch your hands over your head and then brush them down in front of your body, smoothing out your aura and energy field as you brush away heavy, sticky, or dissonant energies.

Be sure to, as much as possible, sense and remove energetic blocks, or other attachments, in your energy field.

Just brush them away if possible. You may have to pull certain things out or use other techniques if karma or learning is involved in releasing lower vibe energies.

2. Second, return your hands above and just behind your head and push down behind your body (*you should generally start at your head, brush down to your shoulders, moving your hands so they are then below your middle back and continue downward below your bum as far as you can easily, gracefully reach*).

Again, use your hands to brush away or remove any sticky or denser energy that you find in your field.

3. Finally, if you have sage, cleanse the energy you have removed with the sage ritual.

If you don't have sage, there is a visualisation-based energy work that you can do.

Visualise your spine energy thrust into the earth, a column of light, and send the dark, low vibes down into the planet and mentally ask that Mother Earth transmute the energies into Divine Light energies, and then thank her for this.

It is vital to maintain your aura and energy field.

Tears and other issues can drain energy and allow unwanted frequencies or beings.

AURIC REPAIR EXERCISE

1. Invoke the essence of the Divine, G-d/Goddess. Ask them to assist you in repairing your aura and energy field.

2. In your mind's eye, scan around your body and being and your entire energy field. When you feel an opening, rip or tear, it might feel spongy, jagged, or somehow not right.

3. Hold your right soul star over the first leak or tear you wish to seal,

with your palm about four or five inches away from your body, with the fingers gently held together straight and the palm flat.

Now slowly move your hand gently over the area where you have detected the leak, tear or other issues.

Allow your inner knowing to help you sense the best way—and at the ideal speed or pace—to move your hand. Don't rush (and relax; you can't get this wrong; aura repair may take a little practice).

4. You can also sew a rip or tear shut; take some energy or Light from the air and create a needle and thread of Light. Use the needle and thread of Light to sew up any rips or tears you see.

Make a complete pass over your entire aura, including behind your back.

Make all needed repairs, then smooth your aura.

5. Then place your awareness on your crown chakra and ask G-d/G-ddess, Source, to flood you with extra Light to re-energize your aura and field.

6. In closing, thank the essence of the Divine, G-d/G-ddess.

7. If you are in a place where you can, do the sage ritual to cleanse up and residual unwanted energies, followed by the grounding ritual.

Protection & Shielding

Shielding, like praying, should be done daily.

It can be simple. The easiest prayer is to ask to be protected, shielded and surrounded by the essence of the Divine Light of G-d/G-ddess, all that is Holy and pure.

When you make prayers, envision, embody and experience—to the greatest degree possible —the meaning of the words. As your clairvoyance increases, you may see and feel flashes of Light or the presence of Divine beings. Though we cannot expect prayer alone to protect or shield us, intention, prayer, chanting, meditation, and the like, are very powerful spiritual tools that impact our realities.

PROTECTION PRAYERS

Stand, arms relaxed at your side, or sit comfortably.

Quick Prayer/Chant

G-d/G-ddess within,
G-d/G-ddess without,
Make a circle of Light all about,
Let Love In, Push evil out.
Thank you, and Amen.

Holy Protection Prayer

I call forth the Essence of Divinity to occupy my physical space, protecting me from negative energies within and without. Surround me with Love and Light, let Love in and push evil out. Thank you, and Amen.

Prayer to G-d/G-ddess:

Essence of G-d/G-ddess above and below, within and without, and all around, interpenetrating all of my cells and all of reality, please provide Divine protection. Amen.

SHIELDING PRAYER

Shielding ritual #1:
Request and visualise shields of Light, either bright white or a silver metallic shimmer, in front, behind, to either side, and diagonally in all directions, above and below, and several feet around you. Say thank you, and amen.

Shielding ritual #2:
Request an impenetrable bubble of the Light from the Essence of G-d/G-ddess to surround you entirely. Say thank you, and amen.

Closing

In our world of increasing war, climate change, economic depression, child abduction, rape, murder, violence and other terrible crimes against humans and humanity, as well as poverty, homelessness, political corruption, starvation and lack of clean water and health care, among other issues, it may sometimes seem like there isn't anything we can do, as individuals, to make a difference.

As far as we can discern, the sole purpose of human existence is to kindle a light of meaning in the darkness of mere being.

~CARL GUSTAV JUNG, *MEMORIES, DREAMS, REFLECTIONS*, CHAPTER 11 (1962)

The Starfish Story, based on *The Star Thrower* by Loren Eiseley (1907-1977)—and personal experiences with countless clients and others—makes it clear that each person can make a difference. It is up to each of us to try, do our best, and, in Carl Jung's words, 'kindle a light' in the darkness of our soul and being.

 While writing his book *The Unexpected Universe*, Loren Eiseley was walking along the ocean in Costabel early one morning. Shortly after a storm had subsided, and as he continued walking, he noticed that thousands of starfish had been washed up on the beach.

Ahead of him was a gigantic rainbow of great perfection shimmering into existence. At the base of the rainbow was a little boy, stooped over and gazing fixedly at an object in the sand. Eventually, he flung the object far beyond the breaking surf.

Eiseley approached him and asked, *'Son, what are you doing?'*

The little boy answered, *'I'm throwing starfish back into the sea because if I don't, they will die.'*

'But there are thousands of starfish. In the larger scheme of things, you won't make much of a difference to all these starfish.'

The little boy looked up at him, stooped down again to pick up another starfish and, gently but quickly, flung it back into the ocean.

'It's going to make a difference to that one', he replied.

Eiseley was embarrassed, uncomfortable with the contrast of the little boy's youthful, innocent love for the living with his own hardened, 'mature' indifference.

He had nothing to say and left. He kept walking on the beach but could not get the picture of the little boy out of his mind.

It was a moment of truth for Eiseley, of deep soul searching and self-confrontation.

In time, the area around his eyes suspiciously damp, he returned to the little star thrower, silently picked up a starfish and spun it far out into the waves.

'I understand,' he said quietly.

'Call me another thrower.'

Together, still under the hues of the rainbow, they spent hours throwing starfish back into the ocean.

It was a task not assumed lightly, for it was men and starfish they sought to save, sensing intuitively that man cannot exist spiritually without reverence for all life and hope.

As you consistently spiritually clear low vibes and cultivate high vibes, meaning illuminate, you <u>will</u> heal your life and help heal the world. Thank you for buying this book and blessing me, all of humanity, Mother Earth and the cosmos with the spiritual clearing work you are doing. My blessings and love to you from the heart.

Jane Hawk

FAQs

Clients have asked versions of the following questions, or the topic has come up in some form (so the answers to those frequently asked questions are below).

How do I know I have demons or am under Psychic attack?

You will feel unwell, usually mentally, emotionally, and energetically, if you are infected with any entity or are under psychic attack. You may sometimes hear (internal audio) voices or commands that are quite atypical for you or otherwise experience demonic contact or attempts to influence you in some way negatively. If you are clairvoyant, if you tune in with your inner eye, you may see the beings—in various forms—whether figures or blobs of colours, often red, black, yellow or green.

Of course, voices may occasionally be your unhealed Parts of Self (subpersonalities) or Inner Children, who are sometimes enraged post-trauma or for other reasons, waking up, thawing, available to heal yet first expressing authentic rage, hate, or similar frequency emotions. Additionally, voices may relate to ET communication or experiences. You must get to know your psyche and whole being to distinguish between what is you, your whole being terrain, and what is not.

Sometimes a person is entirely unaware of such interaction until they relocate to a different geographical area or spend more time alone. Then they will hear things they haven't heard before. However, many people are unaware of the demons, or demonic, and other entities and (-) polarity frequencies they carry.

A person may become aware of demons or entities after being around someone with dark energy. You haven't necessarily picked up an entity or other dark forces, though. A person whom you come into contact with may have negative (-) polarities that elicit your latent dark frequencies. Sometimes one may become aware of abnormal or atypical urges toward food, sex, violence, or other behaviours. You will likely know these impulses do not stem from yourself; they will generally seem unusual. That can be a sign that you've picked up some entities or that someone or several someones are trying to influence you.

Both psychic attack and demon infestation can lead to addictive behaviour, depression, fatigue, and negative (-) polarity emotional material, including despair and suicidal feelings. Generally, you will 'feel' or experience the emotional frequency of all beings you are hosting.

Why do I have demons, and why am I under Psychic attack?

Many people have demons; we've carried them from other incarnations or transferred during karmic trauma or different experiences in this lifetime, and psychic attack (where dark energies, including entities, are transmitted to an unwitting person isn't all that uncommon either. Yet, so much of the darkness we carry are connected to us from parallel life issues that are residual.

Your every word is a curse or blessing.

When people think angry, or possibly evil, thoughts about us or wish us harm... they are cursing us, and we are under psychic attack. Yes, it's more subtle and carries less karma than if they were practising black magic against us, but it is a curse nonetheless. It is so vital for each of us to express our negative (-) polarity material appropriately. Anger should be released in expressive arts, through gestalt or other appropriate depth psychology exercises, or by our punching of a pillow and so on.

Additionally, we generally have so much residual karma from parallel lives that other people we meet may react to us with intensely charged negative emotions, seemingly for no reason. We must clean up the mess and accept our experience with humility and a learning orientation.

What kinds of spiritual clearing issues do most people face?

People are dealing with all kinds of issues, whether they are aware of them or not, including intense karma and Soulular patterns residual from parallel lifetimes (what most people consider as past lifetimes), creation issues, polarity reversal, entities, demons and demon fragments and eggs/egg sacks, ET abduction and implants of control and other devices, psychic attack, hexes, curses, spells, and vows by and toward a person, attachment of other souls (including disembodied spirits), dark forces of different kinds (too numerous to mention, plus occasionally new types of beings not seen previously show up). It is not unusual for people to have multiple Soul fragments in parallel lives or this life to have dissociated Inner Child parts of self.

I can't feel or see anything; why is that, and is the work having any effect?

Not feeling or being unaware of feelings, energy, and shifts from spiritual clearing work may be due to several reasons. You may not be grounded in your body and the now. If I ask you to 'Put your awareness on the top of your head, on your feet, on your back or body, where it's pressed against the furniture you are sitting or lying on, right now', would you be able to truthfully state that you were already wholly present to your current physical/kinesthetic experience?

You probably were not fully aware of your body in reality. We often unground regularly, though grounding is ideal and required for health and all that is good. Also, everyone is sensitive to energy, at differing times, depending upon their groundedness, as well as esoteric factors such as the alignment of planets in the heavens and their particular natural energy sensitivity.

When you are stressed, exhausted, and overworked, it is easy to be ungrounded, making it less likely that you will feel changes or energy shifts. Drinking caffeine, overeating, and other activities also make it difficult to be sensitive to subtle energies.

Also, we each have a unique karmic destiny and Divine expression (what some people call Life Purpose). Your body and being and your intellect, your physical look and experience, your personality, your emotions and energy sensitivity, are all perfect for your karmic destiny and Divine expression. Awareness of subtle energies and parallel realms may not be a big part of your karmic destiny.

It is also true that you are likely to grow increasingly sensitive to subtle energies throughout your lifetime. Like any expertise, sensitivity to energy and energetic shifts can be cultivated and acquired.

Why do people have differing levels of psychic ability?

Each human has a Soul, and it is the nature of the Soul to have subtle energy awareness or psychic abilities; thus, every human has some capacity for psychic experience or awareness. Some people have extensive parallel life experiences where they developed esoteric and psychic abilities, and again, each person has a different karmic destiny and Divine Expression.

Spiritual exercises, including meditation, grounding, being Exquisitely Present to your whole being, fasting, making pilgrimages, yoga, and visiting certain spots on the planet, can help speed up the development of your psychic abilities. Check out the terrific online psychic development courses offered by Psychic Sonia Choquette. You can sign up through her site.

How can I be sure I'm doing this book's exercises correctly?

So much of life is about living life from humility and being humble, intending to evolve toward increasing purity and goodness. If you have set up a space to be with G-d/G-ddess and clear spiritually, have created your altar from this intention, and have approached the work with humility, reverence, gratitude and love, then you are doing it right.

How will I know if something is too difficult for me to handle?

You will know because you or your Inner Child will experience anxiety, terror or fear at being out of your depth. You'll see, hear or otherwise experience something that you know you must seek guidance about. There are many healers and teachers available in life that can help.

How often should I do this spiritual clearing work?

You should do spiritual rituals and clearing daily, even if for five minutes.

It is ideal if you do the work regularly (don't wait til you are in spiritual or energetic pain to spiritually clear or illuminate). The results of the work are cumulative. I have been doing spiritual rituals very nearly daily for many years. Spiritual clearing and evolving spirituality are journeys to be undertaken for multiple lifetimes.

Will I need to do this type of work forever?

Forever is a long time, yet I expect to be doing spiritual work as long as I am a Soul.

Why do some people have many spiritual issues?

Some of us seem to be highly functioning and successful, and others of us are energy sensitive and keep having psychic attacks, dark force entities, or other heavy spiritual issues to deal with. Some people are less grounded and
unaware of the subtler forces affecting them and their lives.

Some people are significantly less energy sensitive by body type and karmic destiny. Some of us have dark karma from multiple lifetimes that we should clean up in this lifetime (if we are willing to do so). Some people have much dark karma that they are ignorant of; others may be disconnected and unaware they are afflicted.

Some people seem superficially successful in some ways but, upon closer scrutiny, have addictions and other patterns of behaviour or issues that reflect material to clear. Suppose you find yourself under frequent psychic attack (and I don't mean being told you are under psychic attack by your expensive psychic, who isn't a shaman and wants you to keep calling her). In that case, you likely need to work with a professional shaman and healer, preferably in person, having one or more full parallel life field clearings.

If you had childhood trauma, particularly ritual or institutional sexual abuse, you likely have major karmic issues. You may need to do ongoing demonic release and related spiritual clearing work for at least several months.

I do, on average, 90 minutes or more of spiritual work, often spiritual clearing, daily and have for years. Sometimes I have spent multiple days doing this work. You must do what is required to be spiritually clear.

If you have memories of Extra-terrestrial abduction or experienced ritual abuse, as noted above, you will likely need to do ongoing work.

Do the work for yourself or with a professional trained and skilled in these areas.

In my experience with myself and my clients, spiritual clearing is ongoing. You may become aware of demons and entities around a particular season because of parallel life issues related to religious holidays, family tragedies, ancestral issues, etc. Problems connected to specific seasons, holidays or dates may arises.

Some issues don't show up for years; they are impacted, or even constellated, at the cellular level. They may not arise until you are ready to deal with them. Clients and I have had physical experiences— including falling, hitting the head, being thrown from a horse, and the like—incidents which stimulated the release of deeper, impacted material from the cellular level.

Take responsibility for your spirituality and spiritual clearing. Get increasingly grounded through yoga or tai chi/chi gong, walking and meditation and eating an ideal diet.

Meditate, develop your intuition, and communicate with G-d/G-ddess daily.

Is this Spiritual Clearing Work Dangerous?

The work is not, in my experience, inherently dangerous.

However, this work can be intense and frightening though the evolution of one's awareness is also often filled with insights, intuitions and inspirations.

You may experience dramatic personality changes. Along your spiritual path, you may have confusion, identity crisis, loss of a sense of purpose and meaning, deep depression, high anxiety, and what you perceive as a mental breakdown or deconstruction of the self (ego), the personality you thought you were.

A daily spiritual practice, and guidance from teachers or spiritual community support, will ground and support you as you awaken and your awareness expands.

Recommended Resources

The journey is expected to be long, yet there is no better time to be alive. Once secret, esoteric knowledge is available to almost all humanity. Numerous resources can help you learn, grow, and transform for the better; the following are a few that are highly recommended on your voyage.

BOOKS

Remarkable Healings: A Psychiatrist Discovers Unsuspected Roots of Mental and Physical Illness by Dr Shakuntala Modi

In the powerful and fascinating book *Remarkable Healings*, Dr Modi presents evidence and case studies from her psychiatric practice where clients, under hypnosis, described past life traumas and inner children, entities, earth-bound or discarnate spirits, and demons, or fragments of these, attached to/within their bodies and energy fields, creating physical, mental and/or emotional problems. The book should inspire you incredibly if you are as heavily afflicted with dark forces as

was this psychiatrist's clients (who each resolved their attachment issues through hypnosis).

What We May Be: Techniques for Psychological and Spiritual Growth by Piero Ferrucci

This rich love-filled book cultivates transcendent and other powerful beneficial states through specific easy-to-perform exercises that comprise a total psychological and spiritual growth system. Providing case studies of therapeutic clients, the author describes how the reader may experience shifts in consciousness and 'resolve seemingly impossible conflicts, redirect aggressive impulses, awaken intuitive and creative powers, develop a strength of will and the sense of personal freedom, and capacity to love' for themselves.

Recovery of Your Inner Child: The Highly Acclaimed Method for Liberating Your Inner Self by Dr Lucia Capacchione

Dr Capacchione teaches how the Inner Child lives within us; the part of us feels emotions and is playful, intuitive, and creative. Usually hidden under our grown-up personas, the Inner Child holds the key to intimacy in relationships, physical and emotional well-being, addiction recovery, and the creativity and wisdom of our inner selves.

Recovery of Your Inner Child is the premier

book that reveals how to have a firsthand experience of your Inner Child—feeling its emotions and recapturing its sense of wonder —by writing and drawing with your non-dominant hand. Expanding on the highly acclaimed technique introduced in The Power of Your Other Hand, here Dr Capacchione shares scores of hands-on activities that will help you to embrace your Vulnerable Child and your Angry Child, find the Nurturing Parent within, and finally discover the Creative and Magical Child that can heal your life.

INTERNET

Online Name of G-d Meditation

The essential Name of G-d, *Havayah,* is the Eternal Being Masculine emanation. This is the Divine power that all of our reality emanates from or said another way, per inner.org, 'the Divine power that continuously brings all of reality into being' (https://www.inner.org/meditate/havayah/havayah.htm). Learn more about Rabbi Ginsberg here: https://www.inner.org/rav. Rabbi Ginsberg's online audio meditation below is a tool to help you focus and meditate upon G-d's name:

mms://ra.colo.idt.net/ginsburgh/eng/med/name.mp3

MEDIA

Does Past Life Regression Work? Listen to an Oprah Winfrey past-life regression discussion with Brian Weiss, M.D., where the Ivy League–trained psychiatrist discusses how he discovered past lives and the power of past-life clearing work *unexpectedly* while using hypnosis with a client whom he was treating in his psychiatry practice in 1980: https://www.oprah.

com/own-super-soul-sunday/how-dr-brian-weiss-went-from-past-life-skeptic-to-expert-video. Dr Weiss is the author of *Many Lives, Many Masters: The True Story of a Prominent Psychiatrist, His Young Patient, and the Past-Life Therapy That Changed Both Their Lives* (and, along with other parallel life clearing training and education, Jane Hawk trained with Dr Weiss in Los Angeles).

Many Lives, Many Masters: The True Story of a Prominent Psychiatrist, His Young Patient, and the Past-Life Therapy That Changed Both Their Lives: https://www.brianweiss.com/about-the-books/many-lives-many-masters/ and https://www.goodreads.com/book/show/59464398-many-lives-many-masters.

Reincarnation - The Millboro Mass Regression Case

The YouTube video at https://www.youtube.com/watch?v=33tflF3t-yE details the Dr Marge Rieder case, where more than thirty-five clients, near Lake Elsinore, California, under hypnosis, recalled details of their life in the same Virginia town during the American Civil War. Dr Rieder, an experimental hypnosis expert, and her camera crew confirmed the hypnotherapy info and revealed how Souls sometimes reincarnate in a group. The Souls incarnating in a collective are commonly known as a Soul group. The book the video is based on is *Mission to Millboro: A Study in Group Reincarnation* by Marge Rieder, PhD. Learn more at http://www.bluedolphinpublishing.com/mission.htm.

About the Author

Jane Hawk is certified and trained in multiple transpersonal psychology approaches, expressive arts, Inner Child and other inner work, Family Constellation work (Hellinger), Psychosynthesis, spiritual and energetic techniques, hypnosis, NLP, parallel life clearing, Soul Memory Discovery, as well as multiple Jungian or Depth Psychology tools like Gestalt, dream and other symbol work, including sand tray or sand play. Clairvoyant, clairaudient and clairsentient is an energy healer, training in multiple meditation techniques and shamanic practices, including soul retrieval, journeywork, and psychopomp  work. Hawk is devoted to teaching Core Clear techniques to help others release the karmic or other whole being material, whatever is held at the cellular and Soulular level, that blocks their manifestation and experience of the Divine. Although, due to increasingly sensitive energy, she no longer works with people one-on-one, she uses her intuitive and other gifts to write books to help others to do their solo spiritual clearing work to release their low or negative (-) frequency vibes and states of consciousness that manifest as life issues. She shares spiritual clearing and other tools so readers can access high-frequency vibes and manifest their heart and Soul's desires as they core clear and vibe your Dream Life! If you core clear then illuminate (fill with the highest vibrations and energies), you can more easily intend, vibe, manifest your heart and Soul's desires, and connect more deeply to G-d/G-ddess.

CHATTER

Jane Hawk's past clients have shared the following testimonials:

The experience that I shared was both uplifting and spiritual. She is able to identify and assist in areas that are both hard to identify and essential to clear. Shifting the way I view the world. ~KH

Thank you for the honesty & the encouraging & kind words. Wakeup call! Thank you!!!!! ~Julia

This was a nice and refreshing experience. She really does what she states she'll do in her presentation! Thanks :-) ~Violett

About the Publisher

EARTH SUN UNION PRESS

We are Earth Sun Union Press, a small publisher committed to creating books to bring joy, energy, and good vibes to your life, to help you expand your awareness and abilities so that you can be your own guru and uplevel your life (however you would like to do so). A small team of creatives, we love life-hacking, writing, and personal transformation! We hope you will love our brand and emerging titles! If you have suggestions, please email us at earthsununion@gmail.com. To your highest evolution and self-loving, healthy, fit, and high-vibe/high-energy life!

Blessings,
Earth Sun Union Press

ABOUT THE PUBLISHER

Earth Sun Union Press
an imprint of eXu Publishing
http://exupublishing.com/

Love to Read?

OTHER BOOKS BY ESU

Earth Sun Union Press offers other self-development and inner work titles, including several Journal to the Self series books and workbooks such as the lined notebook and journal *Raven Totem: Journal to the Self*.

If you are on a journey to increased physical fitness, health, and wellness, you may like to try our quote-filled *120-Day Food & Fitness Tracker Self-Love Fitness Journal: Journal to the Self*. This is the food and exercise journal for you if you are ready to track your fitness and any needed weight loss the old-fashioned way?! Track EVERYTHING you eat and when you move PLUS, this food and exercise journal allows you to track water and other categories such as daily vitamins.

The book includes a daily self-evaluation of how happy you are with your food and exercise, as well as space to track and deal with cravings and a place to describe what will make tomorrow better. The workbook comes in large print size, a small pocket-sized and other sizes, and will be your convenient diary and motivating planner during your next four months or 120 days (a quarter of a year).

SELF
LOVE

120
DAY
FOOD &
FITNESS
TRACKER

Journal to the Self

To review our catalogue of self-help and books, visit our parent publisher website at https://exupublishing.com/ or find our publications wherever fine books are sold. Thank you!

Blessings and love,

Earth Sun Union Press

End Notes By Chapter

FREQUENCY = REALITY

1. *Though many global frequency (GF) issues pertain to childhood or ancestral trauma, psychic attack, energy infection by entities, and so on, sometimes reversed polarity or ongoing energy leakages can be a GF issue.*

GROUNDING

1. Issues with polarity reversal, and dissociative Inner Children and Parts of Self who keep leaving your body, due to fear, is outside the scope of this particular exercise and this book. Reach out to yoru preferred practitioner for Soul Retrieval and Inner Child or other needed work.

BATH AS RITUAL

1. *Young Living's* Feelings Essential Oils Kit contains 12 incredibly powerful blends: Forgiveness, Grounding, Harmony, Hope, Inner Child, Joy, Present Time, Release, SARA, 3 Wise Men, Valor and White Angelica.
2. *Don't overthink the items needed for a spiritual clearing bath ritual; tune into and experiment with what will create a visually and otherwise beautiful and healing experience for you.*

DARK FORCE ENTITY RELEASE

1. In Psychosynthesis we transmute the consciousness of the Lower self, rather than merely merging it with the Higher Self. This work is quite powerful, the book *What We May Be: Techniques for Psychological and Spiritual Growth by Piero Ferrucci* is highly recommended.

RELAX THE BODY

1. Adonai and Shekinah are the equivalent of Divine Father and Mother, or G-d and the feminine Holy Spirit.
2. We stand on our toes, lifting ourselves, as we say Kadosh, Kadosh, Kadosh (Holy, Holy, Holy) lifting our heels off of the floor when we say this, as a symbol that we are being lifted to a higher level as are the heavenly angels, who are said to praise G-d by singing Kadosh, among other prayers, daily.

HEBREW NAME OF G-D MEDITATION

1. 'I Am that I Am' is a standard English translation of the Hebrew phrase אֶהְיֶה אֲשֶׁר אֶהְיֶה (*'ehye 'ăšer 'ehye*; pronounced [ʔehˈje ʔaˈʃer ʔehˈje])– also 'I am who (I) am', 'I will become what I choose to become', 'I am what I am', 'I will be what I will be', 'I create what(ever) I create', or 'I am the Existing One' (Stone).

   Stone, Robert E., II (2000), 'I Am Who I Am', in Eerdmans Dictionary of the Bible. Freedman, David Noel and Myers, Allen C. (eds.).

www.ingramcontent.com/pod-product-compliance
Lightning Source LLC
Chambersburg PA
CBHW040903120626
46551CB00006B/629